JUN 2 0 2012

EXPLORING COUNTRIES

Guatemala

by Kari Schuetz

BELLWETHER MEDIA • MINNEAPOLIS, MN

Note to Librarians, Teachers, and Parents:

Blastoff! Readers are carefully developed by literacy experts and combine standards-based content with developmentally appropriate text.

Level 1 provides the most support through repetition of high-frequency words, light text, predictable sentence patterns, and strong visual support.

Level 2 offers early readers a bit more challenge through varied simple sentences, increased text load, and less repetition of high-frequency words.

Level 3 advances early-fluent readers toward fluency through increased text and concept load, less reliance on visuals, longer sentences, and more literary language.

Level 4 builds reading stamina by providing more text per page, increased use of punctuation, greater variation in sentence patterns, and increasingly challenging vocabulary.

Level 5 encourages children to move from "learning to read" to "reading to learn" by providing even more text, varied writing styles, and less familiar topics.

Whichever book is right for your reader, Blastoff! Readers are the perfect books to build confidence and encourage a love of reading that will last a lifetime!

This edition first published in 2012 by Bellwether Media, Inc.

No part of this publication may be reproduced in whole or in part without written permission of the publisher. For information regarding permission, write to Bellwether Media, Inc., Attention: Permissions Department, 5357 Penn Avenue South, Minneapolis, MN 55419.

Library of Congress Cataloging-in-Publication Data
Schuetz, Kari.
 Guatemala / by Kari Schuetz.
   p. cm. – (Exploring countries) (Blastoff! readers)
 Summary: "Developed by literacy experts for students in grades three through seven, this book introduces young readers to the geography and culture of Guatemala"–Provided by publisher.
 Includes bibliographical references and index.
 ISBN 978-1-60014-618-3 (hardcover : alk. paper)
 1. Guatemala–Juvenile literature. I. Title.
F1463.2.S45 2012
972.81–dc22   2011002224

Printed in the United States of America, North Mankato, MN.

080111   1187

Contents

Mexico

Belize

Gulf
of
Honduras

Guatemala

Honduras

★
Guatemala City

El Salvador

Pacific
Ocean

N
W   E
S

Did you know?
Guatemala comes from a language of the Mayan people. It means "the land of the high trees."

4

Caribbean Sea

Guatemala is the third-largest country in Central America. It covers 42,042 square miles (108,889 square kilometers) between the Pacific Ocean and the Caribbean Sea. Four countries border Guatemala. Mexico is to the west and north. Belize, Honduras, and El Salvador lie to the east. The Gulf of Honduras washes onto the country's short eastern coast. Guatemala City, the capital of Guatemala, is found in the southern part of the country. More people live in Guatemala City than in any other city in Central America.

Lake Atitlán

Did you know?

Lake Atitlán, the deepest lake in Central America, lies in southeastern Guatemala. This beautiful lake's name is Mayan for "the place where the rainbow gets its colors."

Guatemala has coastal plains in the south, highlands in the middle of the country, and a **plateau** in the north. The Sierra Madre span from Guatemala to Mexico. This mountain range includes Tajumulco, the highest point in Central America. The Motagua River, Guatemala's longest river, flows between the Sierra Madre and the Cuchumatanes Mountains. The river empties into the Gulf of Honduras.

The Petén fills the northern third of Guatemala. This **limestone** plateau stretches into the Yucatán **Peninsula**. It includes many **cloud forests** and **tropical rain forests**. Heavy rainfall often leads to floods in this region.

Santa María

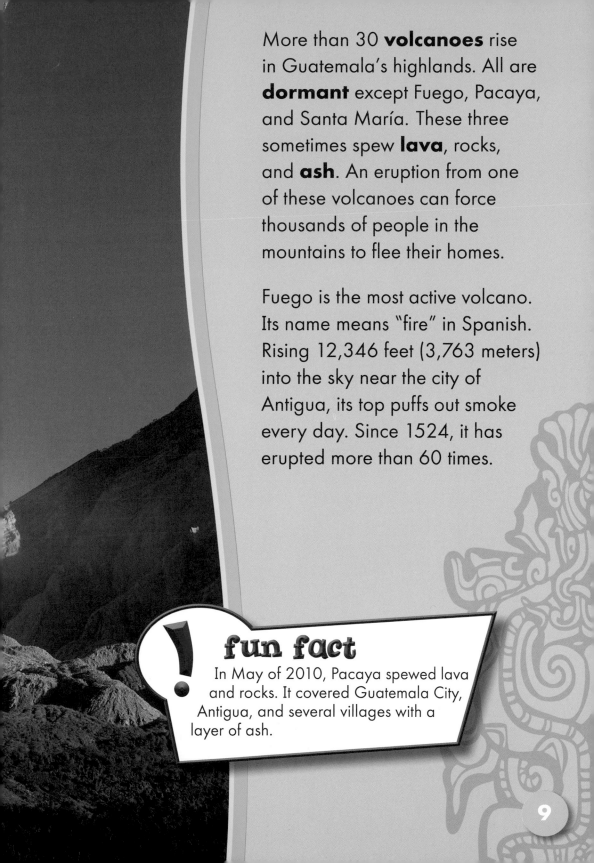

More than 30 **volcanoes** rise in Guatemala's highlands. All are **dormant** except Fuego, Pacaya, and Santa María. These three sometimes spew **lava**, rocks, and **ash**. An eruption from one of these volcanoes can force thousands of people in the mountains to flee their homes.

Fuego is the most active volcano. Its name means "fire" in Spanish. Rising 12,346 feet (3,763 meters) into the sky near the city of Antigua, its top puffs out smoke every day. Since 1524, it has erupted more than 60 times.

fun fact

In May of 2010, Pacaya spewed lava and rocks. It covered Guatemala City, Antigua, and several villages with a layer of ash.

quetzal

Did you know?

Guatemala's national bird is the colorful quetzal. It appears on Guatemala's flag and is also the name of the country's money.

Guatemala is home to many different animals. On the Petén plateau, jaguars, tapirs, and ocelots roam the rain forests and cloud forests. Spider monkeys swing from tree to tree. Howler monkeys make noises that can be heard from miles away. They are one of the loudest animals in the world!

howler monkey

ocelot

vampire bat

! **fun fact**

More than 100 kinds of bats fly throughout Guatemala. Most eat insects, but the vampire bat feeds on the blood of animals!

Long-legged rodents called agoutis scurry through forests. These and other rodents must watch out for beaded lizards and venomous snakes. The jumping viper can strike its prey in mid-air!

Did you know?

Mayan women weave colorful clothing. Traditional Mayan shirts, or *huipils*, look like ponchos. They are worn with long skirts called *cortes*.

More people live in Guatemala than in any other country in Central America. Over 13.5 million people call the country home. Almost half are Mayans. They belong to the Mam, the Quiché, and about 20 other Mayan groups. Most of them live in small villages in the highlands and speak their traditional Mayan languages.

Many *Ladinos* live in Guatemala's cities. These people have both Spanish and Mayan **ancestors**. Some people with African and Caribbean roots live in the southern part of Guatemala. These people speak a language called Garifuna. Guatemala's official language is Spanish.

Speak Spanish!

English	Spanish	How to say it
hello	hola	OH-lah
good-bye	adiós	ah-dee-OHS
yes	sí	SEE
no	no	NOH
please	por favor	POHR fah-VOR
thank you	gracias	GRAH-see-uhs
friend (male)	amigo	ah-MEE-goh
friend (female)	amiga	ah-MEE-gah

About half of all Guatemalans live in the countryside. Many live in the mountains. Houses there are made of grasses, **adobe**, and wood. They often have **thatched** roofs and dirt floors. People trade food and goods within their villages. They sometimes travel to large cities to shop at stores and outdoor markets.

Roads in major cities like Antigua and Guatemala City are usually crowded with trucks, buses, bicycles, and cars. People in the cities live in houses and apartments. Colorful buildings and churches line the streets.

Where People Live in Guatemala

countryside 51%

cities 49%

Children in Guatemala attend six years of primary school. They study science, math, and history. They also learn Spanish and English. At the end of every school year, students take a test. Students who pass move on to the next grade. About one out of every five students chooses to attend secondary school. Students at this level learn specific jobs or prepare for universities. Many Guatemalans study to become teachers, farmers, or business people.

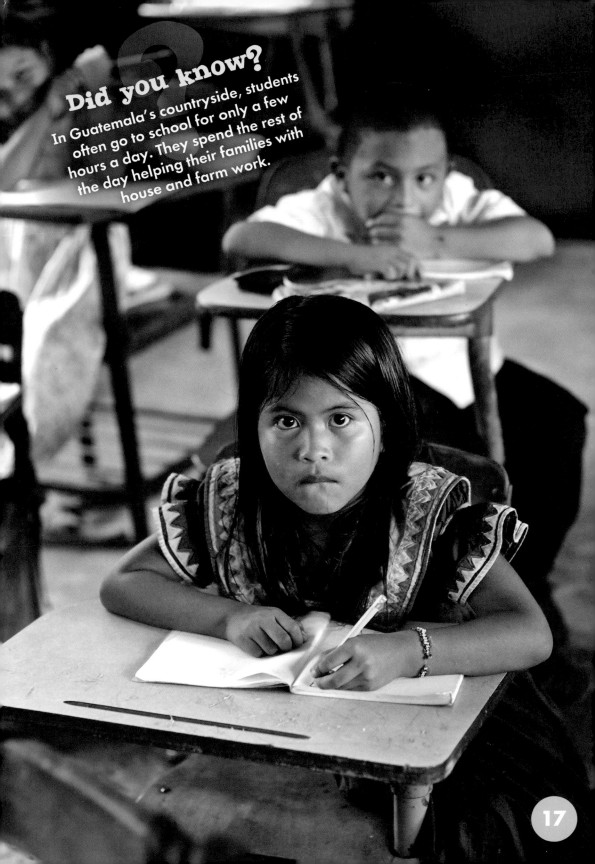

Where People Work in Guatemala

farming 50%

manufacturing 15%

services 35%

Many Guatemalans work as farmers. They grow corn, beans, and squash in the highlands. Along the coastal plains, they raise animals for food and grow coffee beans, sugarcane, and bananas. Some Guatemalans drill into the earth for oil. In the Motagua River Valley, miners dig for **jadeite** and other **minerals**.

Service jobs are plentiful in Guatemala's cities. People work in shops, restaurants, and museums that attract **tourists** from around the world. In cities along the coast, fishermen cast their nets into the Pacific Ocean. They catch shrimp, tuna, mackerel, and other seafood.

Soccer is the favorite sport in Guatemala.
Children often play in open fields and empty
lots after school. Many dream of joining the
national team and competing in the **World Cup**.
Guatemalans also enjoy baseball, basketball,
and boxing.

Guatemala's landscape supports many outdoor activities. People hike the country's many volcanoes or bike up and down the mountains. They snorkel, scuba dive, and surf in the coastal waters of the Pacific Ocean and the Caribbean Sea. Whitewater rafting is common on the Motagua River.

Did you know?
Some people explore the limestone caves of the Petén for fun. This activity is called spelunking.

Did you know?

Guatemalans eat *fiambre* on All Saints' Day and the Day of the Dead. *Fiambre* is a dish made from up to 50 different meats, vegetables, and fish.

Guatemalan food is a mix of Mayan and Spanish flavors. Tortillas, black beans, and rice are served with almost every meal. Corn is a common ingredient in most foods. *Chiles rellenos* is one popular dish in Guatemala. To make it, people stuff peppers with meat and vegetables. Another favorite food is the *tamale*. Guatemalans wrap plantain leaves around *masa*, or dough, to make this dish. They often choose to fill their *tamales* with meat, vegetables, and cheese. Flan and *tres leches* are popular desserts throughout the country. Coffee and *horchata* are favorite beverages. To make *horchata,* Guatemalans add rice, cocoa, and cinnamon to cold milk.

flan

tamales

Semana Santa

Independence Day

Semana Santa is the major religious holiday in Guatemala. It celebrates the holy week that leads up to the Christian holiday of Easter. For *Semana Santa*, people lay colorful carpets made of flowers and plants on the streets of Antigua. They fill the streets to watch religious parades. Another big celebration in Guatemala is *Carnival*. It features parties during the week before the Christian season of **Lent**.

Independence Day, Guatemala's national holiday, takes place on September 15. Guatemalans remember the day in 1821 when they gained their independence from Spain. They gather in the streets for parades and dancing.

The ancient Mayan **civilization** thrived in Guatemala from about 250 to 900 CE. The Mayans were advanced for their time. They wrote in **hieroglyphics** and used complex math. In the 900s, the Mayan civilization started to decline. Spanish explorers came to Guatemala in the 1500s. They found the **ruins** of huge Mayan temples and cities.

fun fact

Many pyramids rise at Tikal. They face each other and allow a person at the top of one pyramid to talk to a person at the top of another!

Tikal, located in the Petén region of Guatemala, once served as a center for the Mayan civilization. Today, people from around the world visit the city's ruins to see how the ancient Mayans lived. Tikal's ruins are a reminder of a people who shaped the vibrant culture of Guatemala.

Fast Facts About Guatemala

Guatemala's Flag

The flag of Guatemala has three vertical stripes. The stripes on the left and right are blue, and the stripe in the middle is white. The blue color stands for the Pacific Ocean, the Caribbean Sea, and the sky. The white stands for peace and purity. Guatemala's coat of arms is in the center of the flag. The quetzal, scroll, rifles, swords, and wreath represent freedom.

Official Name: Republic of Guatemala

Area: 42,042 square miles (108,889 square kilometers); Guatemala is the 106th largest country in the world.

Capital City:	Guatemala City
Important Cities:	Antigua, Quetzaltenango, Escuintla
Population:	13,824,463 (July 2011)
Official Language:	Spanish
National Holiday:	Independence Day (September 15)
Religions:	Christian, traditional Mayan
Major Industries:	farming, fishing, manufacturing, mining, services
Natural Resources:	oil, nickel, gold, silver, iron ore, chicle, jadeite
Manufactured Products:	clothing, furniture, metals, rubber products
Farm Products:	sugarcane, corn, beans, bananas, coffee beans, cardamom, cattle, squash, sheep, pigs, poultry
Unit of Money:	quetzal; the quetzal is divided into 100 centavos.

Glossary

adobe—bricks made of clay and straw that are dried in the sun

ancestors—relatives who lived long ago

ash—fine mineral debris that shoots out of an erupting volcano

civilization—a highly developed, organized society

cloud forests—forests that are often covered in fog

dormant—not active; dormant volcanoes can become active again.

hieroglyphics—pictures that stand for words, phrases, and ideas; the ancient Mayans wrote with hieroglyphics.

jadeite—a mineral that is usually green; jadeite is used to make gemstones and jewelry.

lava—hot, melted rock that flows out of an active volcano

Lent—the forty weekdays before the Christian holiday of Easter

limestone—hard stone that forms over millions of years from old coral and shells

minerals—elements found in nature; gold and silver are examples of minerals.

peninsula—a section of land that extends out from a larger piece of land and is almost completely surrounded by water

plateau—an area of flat, raised land

ruins—the physical remains of a human-made structure

service jobs—jobs that perform tasks for people or businesses

thatched—made from straw, reeds, and other natural materials; the roofs of many houses in Guatemala's countryside are thatched.

tourists—people who are visiting a country

tropical rain forests—thick, green forests that lie in the hot and wet areas near the equator; it rains about 200 days each year in many tropical rain forests.

volcanoes—holes in the earth; when a volcano erupts, hot, melted rock called lava shoots out.

World Cup—an international soccer competition held every four years

To Learn More

AT THE LIBRARY

Croy, Anita. *Guatemala*. Washington, D.C.: National Geographic, 2009.

Morrison, Marion. *Guatemala*. New York, N.Y.: Children's Press, 2005.

Sexton, James D. *Mayan Folktales: Folklore from Lake Atitlán, Guatemala*. New York, N.Y.: Anchor Books, 1992.

ON THE WEB

Learning more about Guatemala is as easy as 1, 2, 3.

1. Go to www.factsurfer.com.

2. Enter "Guatemala " into the search box.

3. Click the "Surf" button and you will see a list of related Web sites.

With factsurfer.com, finding more information is just a click away.

Index

The images in this book are reproduced through the courtesy of: Mark Yarchoan, front cover; Maisei Raman, front cover (flag), p. 28; Alfonso de Tomás, pp. 4-5; Juan Martinez, pp. 5 (small), 11 (bottom), 23 (left, right); Novastock/Photolibrary, pp. 6-7; Edward Parker/Alamy, p. 7 (small); Westend61 GmbH/Alamy, pp. 8-9; Konrad Wothe/Minden Pictures, pp. 10-11; Amazon-Images/Alamy, p. 11 (top); Andy Poole, p. 11 (middle); S Murphy-Larronde/Photolibrary, p. 12; Shawn Talbot, p. 14; Wendy Connett/Photolibrary, p. 15; Kike Calvo/AP Images, pp. 16-17; Frédéric Soreau/Photolibrary, p. 18; Sean Sprague/Photolibrary, p. 19 (left); Sergio Izquierdo/Photolibrary, p. 19 (right); Getty Images, p. 20; Rough Guides/Tim Draper/Glow Images, p. 21; Sergio Pitamitz/Photolibrary, p. 22; Robert Francis/Photolibrary, p. 24; Stefano Paterna/Alamy, p. 25; A. Robert Turner/Alamy, p. 25 (small); Daniel Loncarevic, pp. 26-27; Danita Delimont/Alamy, p. 29.

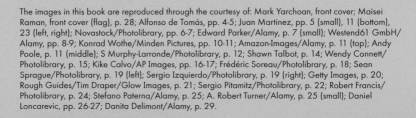